LIVING A MORE
THOUGHTFUL
LIFE

Thinkable Thoughts and
Relevant Reflections

Ervin (Earl) Cobb
Charlotte D. Grant-Cobb, PhD

What Others Are Saying About This Book

"The Cobbs make a solid case that our minds are a bee-hive of activity and are pulled in multiple directions by media, social media, the immediacy of life's pressures and our own pre-conceived biases. We need to learn to slow down and focus - really focus - on unchanging truths. This book helps by culling the essential elements of a career well fulfilled and a life well lived. Very well done."
Kevin J Salcido – Senior HR Executive/People Developer
– Phoenix, Arizona

"I enjoyed the concept of how you came to these thoughts. Yes, they are worth thinking about. The layout almost seemed like one for a class. You might consider offering it. I really resonated with Sunk Cost. Dodge Ball was a new perspective I really liked."
Marti (Weirich) Lorenzen – Retired Human Resources Director
– Queen Creek, Arizona

"I enjoyed the insights you provided in this book. I believe that your reflections can serve as a guide to others looking for answers to many of life's questions."
Angela Phoenix – Realtime Voice Captioner
– Colorado Springs, Colorado

"Earl and Charlotte's latest book is an easy-to-read compendium of great daily thoughts. Simply written, with a workbook page entry for the reader on each thought item, the book is a gem. Given the myriad issues we all face in this too rapidly spinning world, positive helpful thoughts on items like Resilience, Ignorance, and fifty others are highly needed."
Doug Russell – Retired Technology and Project Manager
– Chesterfield, Virginia

"Those who read this book, will want to help make the needed changes."
Alfred Etheredge – Computer Software Professional
– West Palm Beach Florida

What Others Are Saying About This Book

"The concept of neuroplasticity, the brain's ability to modify, change, and adapt both structure and function throughout life and in response to experiences is what jumps off the pages for me. I enjoyed the invitation to capture your own reflections for each chapter."
Dr. Dave Cornelius – Business Executive, Agile coach and Author – Tempe, Arizona

"Ervin (Earl) Cobb and Charlotte Grant-Cobb PhD are knowledgeable and understanding accomplished authors and human beings. Their presence and grace make this a better world. Living a More Thoughtful Life reflects their outstanding contribution towards the enrichment of people's lives and their relationships with others. 'Bravo' to this work, Thank you Ervin and Dr. Charlotte. For me, I enjoyed the invitation to capture my own reflections for each chapter."
James Joseph Waskiel – Measurement and Analysis Engineer – Gadstrup, Denmark

"I highly recommend obtaining the book Living a More Thoughtful Life: Thinkable Thoughts and Relevant Reflections to reflect on your career, personal life, and the highly charged political world that we live in today."
Gus Figueroa – Enterprise/Technology Leadership & Consulting – Tempe, Arizona

"A great deal of useful nuggets that require thought and more thought. In particular, the chapters on Success and You, Listening, and Good Judgement, could spare a young leader some growth pains. Living A More Thoughtful Life would make an excellent graduation or promotion gift."
Jim Grigsby - Semi-retired Management Consultant and Author – Vero Beach, Florida

"The book is stimulating and easy to understand. It covers a lot of life issues including self-examination and happiness wrapped into joy. A good read."
Alexander Williams – Retired Supply Management Professional – Gilbert, Arizona

Other Books By
Ervin (Earl) Cobb And Charlotte D. Grant-Cobb

Why Is It So Hard
Becoming a People Person in the Post COVID-19 Era

Situations and Leadership
Short Stories and Lifelong Lessons

Leadership Front and Center
A Decade of Thought and Tutelage

The SMART LEADER and the Skinny Principles
How to Win and Lead within Any Organization

Driving Ultimate Project Performance
Transforming from Project Manager to Project Leader

**The Official Leadership Checklist and Diary
for Project Management Professionals**

The Leadership Advantage
Do More. Lead More. Earn More.

God's Goodness & Our Mindfulness
Responding versus Reacting to Life Changing Circumstances

Focused Leadership
What You Can Do Today To Become a More Effective Leader

Transition
Solace and Comfort for the Broken Hearted

Pillow Talk Consciousness
Intimate Reflections on America's 100 Most Interesting
Thoughts and Suspicions

Navigating the Life Enrichment Model™

Living a Richer Life
Getting the Most out of Life's Gifts and Circumstances

Until I Change
Affirmations for Mastering Personal Change

Published by RICHER Press
An Imprint of Richer Life, LLC
5710 Ogeechee Road, Suite 200-175, Savannah, Georgia 31405
www.richerlifellc.com

Cover Design: RICHER Media USA
Photographs: Bigstock

The thoughts included are a work of the authors. Names, characters, places and incidents are the product of the author's imagination or are used fictitiously. Any resemblance to actual persons, living or dead, events or locales is entirely coincidental.

Volume book discounts are available for groups, companies and organizations. Contact the publisher for information

Library of Congress Control Number: 2022945004

Living a More Thoughtful Life
Thinkable Thoughts and Relevant Reflections

Ervin (Earl) Cobb and Charlotte D. Grant-Cobb, PhD

1. New Age Thought 2. Mindfulness 3. Communication & Social Skills

(pbk : alk. Paper)

Paperback ISBN: 979-8-9863598-1-6
Also Available in Amazon Kindle eBook - ASIN:B0BC2MZ1RS

PRINTED IN THE UNITED STATES OF AMERICA

"We are what we think. All that we are arises with our thoughts. With our thoughts, we make the world."

— Buddha

CONTENTS

CONTENTS

Thinkable Thoughts and Reflections (cont.)

PREFACE

If the experts are correct, since I started my corporate career as a Systems Engineer with Honeywell in 1975, I have engaged in more than one-trillion and twenty-two million opportunities to earn valued currency.

Unfortunately, this currency is not valued in American dollars.

This number represents the opportunities to earn the "corporate currency" which resided within the 80,000 thoughts I had every day [according to cognitive psychologists] during the 35-years of my successful career in Fortune 100, mid-sized, and venture-funded companies.

My success within all of these organizations was tethered to my willingness to take on difficult challenges, and my ability to earn and maintain the trust of everyone around me.

In my bestselling book that was published in 2019, "*The SMART Leader and the Skinny Principles*", I stated the following:

"*You should think of the <u>trust</u> that your organization has in you as your <u>workplace currency</u>. This is a currency you must use every day to carry out your leadership role and to achieve organizational goals.*"

At some point during my career, it became obvious to me that the opportunities to earn this *workplace currency* actually reside within our levels of thinking, and manifests itself in the "thinkable thoughts" shared daily within the organizations we work and the teams we lead. By "thinkable," I am referring to thoughts that when shared with others can easily be understood, reasoned, and utilized in decision-making and engaging with others on a daily basis.

During the summer of 2021, following months of isolation during the COVID-19 pandemic, and weeks of Zoom meetings, I began to reflect upon some of the *thinkable thoughts* I have shared over the years with co-workers, team members and others. These were thoughts that guided my thinking, and were fundamental to my success and to gaining organizational-wide trust.

As a result, I decided to begin a regiment of taking an hour every week to *ponder* and write down a *thinkable thought.* The aim of each *thought* was to shed light on a valuable lesson-learned from my success in leading and working with others within multiple types and sizes of organizations.

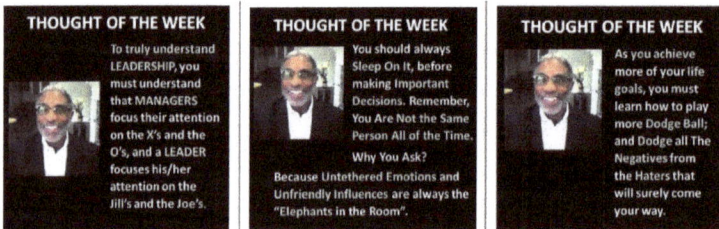

THOUGHT OF THE WEEK
To truly understand LEADERSHIP, you must understand that MANAGERS focus their attention on the X's and the O's, and a LEADER focuses his/her attention on the Jill's and the Joe's.

THOUGHT OF THE WEEK
You should always Sleep On It, before making Important Decisions. Remember, You Are Not the Same Person All of the Time. Why You Ask? Because Untethered Emotions and Unfriendly Influences are always the "Elephants in the Room".

THOUGHT OF THE WEEK
As you achieve more of your life goals, you must learn how to play more Dodge Ball; and Dodge all The Negatives from the Haters that will surely come your way.

However, there was one caveat. Each *thought* had to be crafted from a distinctively humanizing and simplifying perspective, which recognizes the shifts and changes currently taking shape within today's global workplaces.

About twelve months and *fifty-two thoughts* later, I must say that I was gratified with the thoughts I produced.

But, then I began to grapple with the following:

- In today's world of global and instant communications, driven by social media and the difficulty associated with identifying an audience whose attention span exceeds 280 characters —*with whom should I share these thoughts?*

- Also, what are the risks versus rewards of *"giving back"* and sharing some of my hard-earned and well-spent corporate currency?

During these deliberations, I remembered a *thought* on the topic of *"giving back"* credited to General Colin Powell, statesman, diplomat, and United States Army officer who served as America's 65th Secretary of State.

General Powell once stated: *"Giving back involves a certain amount of giving up."*

After discussions with some of my most trusted coaching and career development associates , I soon began to agree that those who were given the opportunity to have access to my "thinkable thoughts" and who took the time to consciously reflect upon them, would greatly benefit — and the rewards will overshadow the risks.

With the insightful and supportive assistance of my wife of forty years, Dr. Charlotte Grant-Cobb, the book you are about to read contains the fifty-two *thinkable thoughts* as well as fifty-two *relevant reflections*. We believe that each of the *thoughts* and *reflections* can help illuminate and reinforce your path to *living a more thoughtful life*.

Earl

"Thinking is the hardest work there is, which is probably the reason why so few engage in it."

— Henry Ford

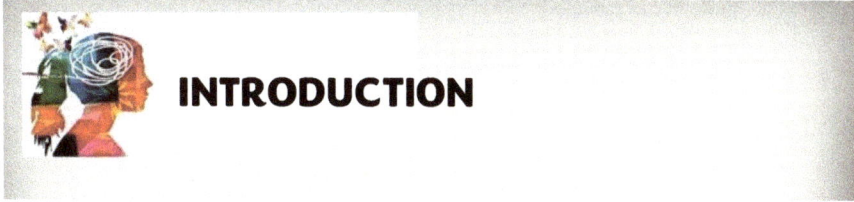

INTRODUCTION

WHY TAKE THIS JOURNEY

Experts estimate that the human mind thinks between 60,000 to 80,000 thoughts a day. This staunch reality is incredible, and can be overwhelming. What's more concerning is that research has shown that the human mind, more often than not, takes *cognitive shortcuts* to help us make some of life's most important decisions. These shortcuts can lead to *implicit* or *unconscious* bias, and in many cases, lost opportunities for personal, professional and financial growth.

WHAT YOU WILL FIND IN THIS BOOK

In this book, we share and shed light on fifty-two *"thinkable thoughts."* By "thinkable," we are referring to insightful thoughts that ignite one's imagination and can easily be regarded as conceivable, feasible and beneficial in many aspects of your personal and professional life.

The *thoughts* we have included in this book constitute a *way of thinking*, that our experiences have taught us to be valuable in decision-making and engaging with others. Each of the *thoughts* are crafted to provide a distinctively *humanizing* and *simplifying* approach to gaining a broader perspective on some of the most common challenges we all face today within a contentious, competitive, social media-driven, and unforgiving society. Societal challenges that can be conquered and transformed into opportunities by simply *living a more thoughtful life.*

HOW WILL YOU BENEFIT

The benefits you will receive from the time you spend reading and digesting the *thoughts* and *reflections* will ultimately depend upon you.

If you just enjoy reading this book, and pick up a few nuggets of insight, you will find yourself *ahead of the pack* when facing one of the challenges associated with the *thoughts* and *reflections*.

If you take the time to *ponder* and execute a plan that will help you integrate the essence surrounding each *thought* into how you *see the world* on a daily basis, we believe that you will benefit greatly from this inspiring and strengthening mental exercise.

Most experts agree that practicing a new and challenging mental activity like this is also a good way of building and maintaining strong cognitive skills.

According to Dr. John N. Morris, director of social and health policy research at the Harvard-affiliated Institute for Aging Research:

> *"Your brain has the ability to learn and grow as you age — a process called brain plasticity — but for it to do so, you have to train it on a regular basis. Eventually, your cognitive skills will wane and thinking and memory will be more challenging, so you need to build up your reserve. Embracing a new activity that also forces you to think and learn and requires ongoing practice can be one of the best ways to keep the brain healthy."*

In either case, by spending some time with this book, you will benefit, and move a little closer to *living a more thoughtful life*.

LEADING CHANGE

"The only constant in life is change.

You should make sure you lead it, and not become a victim of it.

Because those who simply follow change, will find it difficult to gain commitment and value the ultimate outcome."

Thinkable Thoughts and Reflections

Reflecting Upon
LEADING CHANGE

"Be the change you wish to see in the world."
— Mahatma Gandhi

An Indian lawyer, anti-colonial nationalist and political ethicist who employed nonviolent resistance to lead the successful campaign for India's independence from British rule.

Leading as much of the change that occurs in your life as possible, should be an ultimate goal. However, to lead change you must be authentic, inspirational, visible, Inclusive, clear, proactive, educational, measured, reinforcing, and evolving.

Your Thoughts...

_____

_____

_____

_____

_____

_____

_____

_____

_____

Your Responsiveness

"When professionally networking within social media platforms, no response, when one is warranted, speaks louder than anything you can possibly say."

Thinkable Thoughts and Reflections

Reflecting Upon
YOUR RESPONSIVENESS

"Not responding is a response."
— Jonathan Carroll
    An American fiction writer primarily known for novels that may be labelled magic realism, slipstream or contemporary fantasy.

One of the most powerful things you can say to someone else isn't actually a word. It's not even a gesture. It's simply nothing. You should be aware of all of your forms of communications.

Your Thoughts...

_____

_____

_____

_____

_____

_____

_____

_____

_____

YOUR HEALTH

"Your number one priority should be good health. You can make money and capture Social Media Likes.

But, if you do not take care of yourself and your health, it can be all over in an instant."

Thinkable Thoughts and Reflections

Reflecting Upon

YOUR HEALTH

"The first wealth is health."
— Ralph Waldo Emerson
    An American essayist, lecturer, philosopher, and poet.

Your health is at the center of your life. Every part of your life
relies on you having good health. You can have all the riches
and success in the world, but if you don't have your health, you
have nothing.

Your Thoughts...

_____

_____

_____

_____

_____

_____

_____

_____

DEALING WITH DEFEAT

"It's not a defeat that keeps you down, it's being demoralized by defeat that keeps you down.

If you learn from a defeat, you will keep coming back...and you will succeed."

Thinkable Thoughts and Reflections

Reflecting Upon

DEALING WITH DEFEAT

"Victory has a thousand fathers, but defeat is an orphan."
— John F. Kennedy
   The 35th President of the United States.

There are only a few things in life that are certain, such as change.

However, there is one thing we know for sure - at some point in life, we are bound to feel defeated and deeply disappointed. The key is to learn the lesson and try again.

Your Thoughts...

_____

_____

_____

_____

_____

_____

_____

_____

_____

YOUR CONSCIOUS DESIRE

"It is true. Because of how the human mind works, you know far less about yourself than you feel you do.

Therefore, you should periodically and sincerely interrogate your conscious thoughts and beliefs.

Then, detach yourself from those...that are not of your conscious desire."

Reflecting Upon
YOUR CONSCIOUS DESIRE

"You know far less about yourself than you feel you do."
— Daniel Kahneman
A Notable Israeli American psychologist, economist, and the 2002 Nobel Memorial Prize winner in Economic Sciences.

Our conscious desires are the reasons behind everything we do.

They are the foundations of all our achievements. They are some of those intangibles that make us tick. However, we must make sure that they are "our" desires and not some that our mind has inadvertently adopted.

Your Thoughts...

_____

_____

_____

_____

_____

_____

_____

_____

_____

TESTS AND TEMPTATIONS

"Both your personal and professional life are full of tests and temptations.

As you navigate these challenges, remember that tests may make your life better and temptations can make your life a bummer."

Thinkable Thoughts and Reflections

Reflecting Upon

TESTS AND TEMPTATIONS

"Temptations, unlike opportunities, will always give you many second chances."
— Orlando Aloysius Battista
   A Canadian American chemist and author.

We can either accept life's challenges and meet them head-on, or we can resist them and wish they just go away. Challenges are woven into the fabric of our lives. They are the tests we all have to face daily. Temptations are also everywhere, but they are avoidable.

Your Thoughts...

_____

_____

_____

_____

_____

_____

_____

_____

LONELY AT THE TOP

"Yes. I have been there, and it does get lonely at the top.

However, the person who walks alone, personally or professionally is a person without a God."

Thinkable Thoughts and Reflections

Reflecting Upon

LONELY AT THE TOP

"You cannot be lonely if you like the person you're alone with."
— Wayne Dyer
    An American self-help author and a motivational speaker.

Faith speaks the language of the heart. It is an expression of hope that goes beyond the conscious mind. Faith gives us strength and the inner resolve to withstand loneliness and turmoil.

Your Thoughts...

_____

_____

_____

_____

_____

_____

_____

_____

_____

SUCCESS and You

"After a thirty-four-year
corporate career and
twelve years of life after,
I have learned that
success is not about
where you work but about
who you are and what
you do."

Thinkable Thoughts and Reflections

Reflecting Upon

SUCCESS and You

"Success is not the key to happiness. Happiness is the key to success. If you love what you are doing, you will be successful."
— Albert Schweitzer
   A Theologian, musician, philosopher and Nobel Prize-winning physician.

The underlying meaning of success, and, ultimately, the way most people perceive it is deeply flawed .We wrongly equate success with achievement and arriving at a destination or attaining a goal. The essence of **success** is the journey and the pleasure of the stops along the way.

Your Thoughts...

_____

_____

_____

_____

_____

_____

_____

_____

LEADERSHIP FOCUS

"To truly understand leadership, you must understand that managers focus their attention on the X's and the O's, and a leader focuses his or her attention on the Jill's and the Joe's. "

Thinkable Thoughts and Reflections

Reflecting Upon

LEADERSHIP FOCUS

"A leader is one who knows the way, goes the way, and shows the way."
— John C. Maxwell
   An American author, speaker, and pastor who has written many books, primarily focusing on leadership.

Leading people is about mobilizing and optimizing the talent and skills of others in order to achieve results. Leading is about motivating and influencing the behavior of others. You manage tasks and lead people.

Your Thoughts...

_____

_____

_____

_____

_____

_____

_____

_____

_____

FOOLISHNESS

"Being a fool (a person who acts unwisely or imprudently) among fools does more than fortify your sense of belonging; It also fortifies your foolish beliefs, your foolish perspectives and your foolish behaviors."

Thinkable Thoughts and Reflections

Reflecting Upon
FOOLISHNESS

"An intelligent man is sometimes forced to be drunk to spend time with his fools."
— Ernest Hemingway
  An American novelist, short-story writer, and journalist.

Foolish people are self-involved, overly optimistic and unable to see their own vulnerabilities. They assume they already know all that needs to be known and see this as a way to "fit in" or to "belong." Although a sense of belonging is fundamental to the way humankind organizes itself, the first step to a permanent state of belonging is to know, and to be your unfoolish self.

Your Thoughts...

_____

_____

_____

_____

_____

_____

_____

_____

_____

TWO SIDES

"Believe it or not, there are always two sides to every story.

Unfortunately, the way the Human Mind works, it follows the rule of what you see is all there is.

Since we can't always see the rest of the story... We should always take the time to look for it, and not simply depend on our Intuition.

By doing so, it could save you time, money, embarrassment, and/or a meal of crow".

Thinkable Thoughts and Reflections

Reflecting Upon
TWO SIDES

"Life and death are one thread, the same line viewed from different sides."
— Lao Tzu
   An Ancient Chinese philosopher and writer.

Intuition can be thought of as insight that arises spontaneously without conscious reasoning. Intuitive decisions can have some serious drawbacks. You might not have fully considered all the alternatives, and therefore have missed an even better solution. It is always worth listening to or trying to understand all sides of a given situation. What you initially see, may not be all there is.

Your Thoughts...

_____

_____

_____

_____

_____

_____

_____

_____

_____

LISTENING

"It's amazing how differently we can SEE an issue when we really LISTEN. However, most of us do not realize that HEARING is just the start of the listening process. Listening requires a <u>humble</u> understanding, reflection, and respect for the thoughts and <u>lives</u> of others.

Active Listening leads to a wider vision, deeper empathy, and more kindness. While simply HEARING serves only as a PAUSE...to then speak passionately and loudly about narrow aspects of much broader issues."

Thinkable Thoughts and Reflections

Reflecting Upon
LISTENING

"I like to listen. I have learned a great deal from listening carefully. Most people never listen."
— Ernest Hemingway
   An American novelist, short-story writer, and journalist.

Listening is more than just hearing the words someone is saying. *Truly listening* is about understanding the "context" in which words are shared, along with other verbal and nonverbal cues. The cues can be in the form of voice inflections, tone, facial expressions and body language. *Empathetic listening* requires the use of your ears, your eyes and your heart.

Your Thoughts...

_____

_____

_____

_____

_____

_____

_____

_____

_____

VIRAL MOMENTS

"TikTok, Facebook, Instagram,
YouTube and Twitter <u>would not</u>
Succeed without Content, Curiosity
and Connections...neither do Careers,
Coping Skills and Civility.

Without being Global Juggernauts, and
within Our Own Skin, we can all create
Millions of Viral Moments...that build
strong Careers, enhance Coping Skills,
and aid in the Cerebral Process of
becoming more Responsible and Civil
human beings. Amen (or so be it)."

Thinkable Thoughts and Reflections

Reflecting Upon

VIRAL MOMENTS

"It's very easy to make a viral video, but longevity and consistency, that's hard."
— Michelle Phan

An American beauty YouTuber. Founder and Owner of the multimillion-dollar cosmetics line EM Cosmetics.

Being comfortable in your skin doesn't mean you have to stay complacent with yourself or not value viral moments. It means you have the confidence in yourself to deal with the "ups" and the "downs" while accepting things as they are. This level of confidence plays a crucial role in your *consistency* and your *longevity* in both your personal and professional endeavors.

Your Thoughts...

_____

_____

_____

_____

_____

_____

_____

_____

INTELLIGENCE OR WISDOM

"When a decision is in doubt, seek Intelligence or Wisdom? Intelligence delivers INSIGHT based on an ability to think logically. While Wisdom offers COMFORT and a grasp of human nature, which is paradoxical, contradictory, and subject to continual change.

If the decision only involves THINGS...choose Intelligence. If the decision involves PEOPLE...seek Wisdom. Remember, Wisdom is about more than just having knowledge – it pulls in one's objective judgment and evaluated experience."

Thinkable Thoughts and Reflections

Reflecting Upon

INTELLIGENCE OR WISDOM

"The only true wisdom is in knowing you know nothing."
— Socrates

   A Greek philosopher from Athens who is credited as the founder of Western philosophy and among the first moral philosophers of the ethical tradition of thought.

Some people have an enormous amount of knowledge, but lack the wisdom needed to cope with daily tasks - *more intelligence and less wisdom.* On the other hand, there are those who are highly efficient in solving complicated issues but don't have the factual knowledge to support their ideas - *more wisdom and less intelligence.*

Your Thoughts...

_____

_____

_____

_____

_____

_____

_____

_____

_____

YOUR STORY

"You must Indulge in and loudly Identify with your own <u>Brand</u> and Not Accept the <u>Labels</u> others may Give You.

Why You Ask?

Because your <u>Brand</u> is truly who you Are or who you Aspire To Be.

The <u>Labels</u> of others represent Who or What they Want you to be.

Unless you tell Your own Story, others will Do It For You."

Thinkable Thoughts and Reflections

Reflecting Upon
YOUR STORY

"A brand for a company is like a reputation for a person. You earn reputation by trying to do hard things well."
— Jeff Bezos

An American entrepreneur, media proprietor, investor, computer engineer, and commercial astronaut. He is the founder, executive chairman and former president and CEO of Amazon.

Protecting your personal brand essentially means protecting your reputation. Your story matters because it is uniquely your own, and no one can tell it the way you can. Remember, if you don't tell your story, someone else will tell their version.

Your Thoughts...

_____

_____

_____

_____

_____

_____

_____

_____

_____

A BAD HAND

"What Should You Do when Life Deals You a Bad Hand?

 Of course, You Play the Hand You are Dealt.

However, it's always wise to Stop... and Make Sure You Understand the Game.

Rules Do Change...and Not Everyone Gets the Notice."

Thinkable Thoughts and Reflections

Reflecting Upon

A Bad Hand

"Good luck is when opportunity meets preparation, while bad luck is when lack of preparation meets reality."
— Eliyahu Goldratt
   An Israeli business management guru who was the originator of the *Optimized Production Technique,* the *Theory of Constraints,* and *Thinking Processes.*

The one constant in life is change. Sometimes we get so caught up in fighting change that we put off actually dealing with it. Big changes in your career or your life require coping skills. Coping skills help you tolerate, minimize, and deal with stressful situations in life.

Your Thoughts...

_____

_____

_____

_____

_____

_____

_____

_____

_____

COMPROMISE

"Compromise is a Power like no other.

However, it involves both Emotional Control and an Empathetic Line of Sight.

This 'Give and Take', starts within the cradle of Strong Minds and ends in the embrace of Honest Hearts."

Thinkable Thoughts and Reflections

Reflecting Upon

COMPROMISE

"A good compromise, a good piece of legislation, is like a good sentence, or a good piece of music. Everybody can recognize it."
— Barack Obama
   The 44th president of the United States.

A good compromise is the fairest compromise which can be reached under the circumstances. Compromises can be used in virtually any setting. Compromising is an essential tool for seeking common ground. However, it does require good communications skills and the ability to recognize "center-field."

Your Thoughts...

_____

_____

_____

_____

_____

_____

_____

_____

CORPORATE INCLUSION

"Corporate <u>Inclusion</u> should be a <u>No Brainer</u>, and not an <u>Occupation</u>. No one wakes up in the morning thinking, I am White, I am African American, I am Latino American, or I am Asian American.

Unfortunately, it's <u>Others</u> who have those thoughts. <u>Race</u> is simply a <u>Cultural Intervention.</u>

Unfortunately, without a society willing to honestly face this reality...everyone loses out on what could have been."

Thinkable Thoughts and Reflections

Reflecting Upon

CORPORATE INCLUSION

"Corporate culture matters. How management chooses to treat its people impacts everything - for better or for worse."
— Simon Sinek
   A British-American author and inspirational speaker.

Your individuality is the best part of yourself. Every person is known by his or her character, thoughts, mindset, and uniqueness. However, *inclusion* demands empathy, and adjustments to your thoughts and mindset, to accommodate those of others.

Your Thoughts...

_____

_____

_____

_____

_____

_____

_____

_____

INDIVIDUALITY

"An Honest Assessment of Human Potential is not the place to express Individuality.

Why you ask?

Because decades of studies have proven that an Individual's *(sometimes psychologically masked)* Bias, Prejudices, and Preferences distort Judgement...and promote Exclusion and not Inclusion."

Thinkable Thoughts and Reflections

Reflecting Upon

INDIVIDUALITY

"The will to win, the desire to succeed, the urge to reach your full potential... these are the keys that will unlock the door to personal excellence."
— Confucius
  A Chinese philosopher and politician of the Spring and Autumn period.

Human potential is the innate ability of every person to live and perform in alignment with their highest self. Objectively assessing potential and identifying an individual's ability to succeed is difficult and requires "objective" and not "subjective" thinking or thinking based on the personal perspective or preferences.

Your Thoughts...

_____

_____

_____

_____

_____

_____

_____

_____

_____

GOOD JUDGEMENT

"Most Experts Agree that Good Judgement is more about Who You Are than What You Know.

However, it's hard to Judge Reality and Truth when you do not Know Yourself."

Thinkable Thoughts and Reflections

Reflecting Upon

GOOD JUDGEMENT

"Judgement comes from experience, and experience comes from bad judgement."
— **Simon Bolivar**
   A Venezuelan soldier and statesman who played a central role in the South American independence movement.

Judgement and insight are vital parts of everyday life. Good judgement includes considering the consequences of one's decisions, thinking before acting and speaking, and having the tools to make good decisions in a variety of situations. Poor judgement occurs when thoughts and beliefs are not consistent with reality.

Your Thoughts...

_____

_____

_____

_____

_____

_____

_____

_____

_____

OUR PAST

"As we continue to fight many of the battles in 2022 that were first fought in 1922, what does this tell us about our past, and about the snakes in the grass?"

Thinkable Thoughts and Reflections

Reflecting Upon
OUR PAST

"To fight and conquer in all our battles is not supreme excellence; supreme excellence consists in breaking the enemy's resistance without fighting."
— Sun Tzu
  A Chinese military general, strategist, philosopher, and writer.

Our future will always contain remnants of our past — *people*, *issues* and *attitudes*. One of the most difficult things we all must learn is that regardless of who we are and our position, we must take the time to know our enemies, pick the battles we can win, and wait for the optimum *time*, *place* and *method*, to fight the others.

Your Thoughts...

_____

_____

_____

_____

_____

_____

_____

_____

_____

THE ELEPHANTS IN THE ROOM

"You should always <u>Sleep On It</u>, before making Important Decisions.

Remember, You Are Not the Same Person All of the Time.

Why You Ask?

Because Untethered Emotions, Unconscious Bias and Unfriendly Influences are always the Elephants in the Room."

Thinkable Thoughts and Reflections

Reflecting Upon

THE ELEPHANTS IN THE ROOM

"An expert is someone who has succeeded in making decisions and judgements simpler through knowing what to pay attention to and what to ignore."
— Edward de Bono

A Maltese physician, psychologist, author, inventor and philosopher who originated the term lateral thinking and wrote the book *Six Thinking Hats.*

By taking the time to relax and clear your mind, you significantly improve the probability of "knowing what to pay attention to and what to ignore" prior to making important decisions. Also, you can eliminate making emotional, hasty and regretful decisions.

Your Thoughts...

_____

_____

_____

_____

_____

_____

_____

_____

_____

UNSOLVED PROBLEMS

"You can't Redefine a Real Problem.

It is what it is.

However, an Unsolved Problem can Redefine You, and the Answer Does Not Reside in the What, but the Why."

Thinkable Thoughts and Reflections

Reflecting Upon

UNSOLVED PROBLEMS

"The game of life is a lot like football. You have to tackle your problems, block your fears, and score your points when you get the opportunity."
— Lewis Grizzard
   An American writer and humorist/Sports editor for the Atlanta Journal.

Realistically defining problems leads to more timely solutions. The process starts with you getting beyond your intuition and beliefs, and then objectively asking the right set of questions. In most cases, by focusing on the "why" and not just the "what" you will provide a short cut to more effective and permanent resolutions.

Your Thoughts...

_____

_____

_____

_____

_____

_____

_____

_____

_____

SUNK COST

"Avoiding a Good Opportunity because of an Unjustified Fear can be Incredibly Costly.

The Result may be 'Sunk Cost' or Future Reward that may Never be Recovered."

Reflecting Upon
SUNK COST

"Nothing is more expensive than a missed opportunity."
— H. Jackson Brown, Jr.

An American author who was best known for his inspirational book, *Life's Little Instruction Book.*

Every day of our lives we are faced with a myriad of opportunities. Missed opportunities often surface after the event. The guilt of the missed opportunity comes swiftly afterwards. We should not lose *good* opportunities and allow *unjustified fear* to win. All of the preparation and investment associated to capture a specific opportunity is most likely a *sunk cost* and not recoverable.

Your Thoughts...

_____

_____

_____

_____

_____

_____

_____

_____

_____

LIFE AND CAREERS

"Life is Messy and Unpredictable; and so are Professional Careers.

Therefore, it is Wise to Focus as much Attention to Constructing Your Career...as You Do to Living Your Life."

Thinkable Thoughts and Reflections

Reflecting Upon

LIFE AND CAREERS

"Your personal life, your professional life, and your creative life are all intertwined."
— Skylar Grey
  An American singer, songwriter, and record producer.

Enjoyable careers can be evasive, but available for the taking. Working to achieve your goals with a *laser focus* is a critical part of constructing successful careers and lives. Then, determining how your personal and professional life can successfully complement each other, will help to "break the code" associated with opening doors to great careers and amazing lives.

Your Thoughts...

_____

_____

_____

_____

_____

_____

_____

_____

_____

GREAT SUCCESS

"Success is a combination of talent, hard work, perseverance and <u>good</u> luck.

Great Success is a combination of talent, hard work, perseverance and <u>great</u> luck."

Thinkable Thoughts and Reflections

Reflecting Upon

GREAT SUCCESS

"The price of success is hard work, dedication to the job at hand, and the determination that whether we win or lose, we have applied the best of ourselves to the task at hand."
— Vince Lombardi
   An American football coach and executive in the National Football League (NFL).

Humanity is united in the passion for success. Perhaps, there is no emotional feeling that is commonly shared among humankind than the passion for success. However, a major success requires a major effort, and sometimes a stroke of good luck.

Your Thoughts...

_____

_____

_____

_____

_____

_____

_____

_____

_____

DODGE BALL

"As you achieve more of your life goals, you must learn how to play more Dodge Ball...

...and Dodge all The Negatives from the Haters that will surely come your way."

Thinkable Thoughts and Reflections

Reflecting Upon

DODGE BALL

"I always tell young girls, surround yourself with goodness. I learned early on how to get the haters out of my life."
— Michelle Obama

An American attorney and author who served as first lady of the United States from 2009 to 2017.

Just as the air we breathe, haters are everywhere. Regardless of your position in life, you will be surrounded by people who use negative and critical comments as well as obnoxious behavior to bring another person down. Simply surround yourself with positive people, and loads of positive thoughts.

Your Thoughts...

_____

_____

_____

_____

_____

_____

_____

_____

_____

THE WORLD IN OUR HEAD

"The world in our heads is not a precise replica of reality.

Our expectations about events are distorted by the <u>pervasiveness</u> and <u>emotional intensity</u> of the influences to which we are exposed."

Thinkable Thoughts and Reflections

Reflecting Upon

THE WORLD IN OUR HEAD

"We live in a fantasy world, a world of illusion. The great task in life is to find reality."
— Iris Murdoch
   An Irish and British novelist and philosopher.

Reality is not always what we think. We all see reality through personal lens shaped by our beliefs, culture, religion, biases, and experiences. Additionally, our mind attempts to protect us by prioritizing our intuition over the need for deep thought and objective analysis. These are cognitive distortions that can affect our capacity to be mindful and may result in misguided decisions.

Your Thoughts...

_____

_____

_____

_____

_____

_____

_____

_____

_____

RIGHT AND WRONG

"Public Apathy, Fear, Ignorance and Disappointment is what the Ruling Class factor into their strategy to win their version of Right and Wrong.

Beware of the strategies of others and keep your vision of Right and Wrong close to your heart and deep in your mind."

Thinkable Thoughts and Reflections

Reflecting Upon

RIGHT AND WRONG

"Right and wrong are not relative terms. There are fundamental truths. Evil flourishes, but good men continue to battle it - and win."
— Mike Gallagher
   An American politician who served as the U.S. representative for Wisconsin's 8th congressional district.

Since there is no scientific instrument that measures moral rightness or wrongness, we must decide what is reasonable to embrace and believe. If we have never thought about "why" we think some actions are good and others are bad, we could be vulnerable to following the vision and the vices of others.

Your Thoughts...

_____

_____

_____

_____

_____

_____

_____

_____

_____

Humanity and Insanity

"As we all remember the unfortunate attack on the U.S. Capital on January 6th 2021...let's think about what it will take to increase the HUMANITY and decrease the INSANITY of a Nation of mostly loving people."

Thinkable Thoughts and Reflections

Reflecting Upon

Humanity and Insanity

"Love and compassion are necessities, not luxuries. Without them humanity cannot survive."
— Dalai Lama

The 14th Dalai Lama, known as Gyalwa Rinpoche is the current Dalai Lama. The highest spiritual leader and former head of the state of Tibet.

Humanity means helping others at times when they need that help the most. Increasing the level of humanity requires a change in human behavior. From behaviors of indifference to behaviors that care for other humans because of a profound conviction that life is better than death, and that to live well means being treated humanely in relationships of mutual respect.

Your Thoughts...

_____

_____

_____

_____

_____

_____

_____

_____

_____

THINK FIRST

"Think First and Then Speak.

This idiom is more than an axiom.

Following this Bit of Wisdom can be the difference between you being perceived as a GIANT of Gray Matter or a TWERP to be Tolerated.

If you Know the Answer, Speak with Authority.

If you Do Not Know the Answer, simply Ask the Right Question.

Inquisitiveness is always Viewed as a Virtue."

Thinkable Thoughts and Reflections

Reflecting Upon
THINK FIRST

"It is better to keep your mouth closed and let people think you are a fool than to open it and remove all doubt."
— Mark Twain

Samuel Langhorne Clemens, known by his pen name Mark Twain, was an American writer, humorist, entrepreneur, publisher, and lecturer.

Here are some basics. The next time you have a conversation with someone, focus entirely on what that person is saying. Then, pause and think about what's most important for you to say, as well as, why you should say it at this time. At this point, it's time for you to speak purposefully and intelligently.

Your Thoughts...

_____

_____

_____

_____

_____

_____

_____

_____

PROCEDURE VS PURPOSE

"You shouldn't allow Procedure to dwarf Purpose. A Procedure is only a series of steps, proven to be one way to achieve a goal.

If Purpose motivates you, remember that the objective is to Resolve to Accomplishment and not Referee to Resentment.

When it comes to guiding human accomplishments, Procedure has its limits.

Sometimes, Nonconformity and Originality can yield the best results."

Reflecting Upon
PROCEDURE VS PURPOSE

"Fresh, innovative thinking is essential for business [and personal] growth, and most people—not just a few gifted "visionaries"—are capable of it."
— Adam Grant

An American popular science author, and professor at the Wharton School of the University of Pennsylvania specializing in organizational psychology.

Innovative thinking and originality results in ideas that no one else will ever be able to replicate, as they cannot look at it through your eyes. Originality can be viewed as a concept. It combines our creativity and individual perspective to solve problems and to manage situations.

Your Thoughts...

_____

_____

_____

_____

_____

_____

_____

_____

_____

PAYING ATTENTION

"The Art of Paying Attention may seem Insignificant. However, Clarity and Success in both your Professional and Personal Life can depend upon your level of awareness.

Through their choice of Words, Posture and even Silence, most people will Unknowingly provide a Tsunami of insight regarding WHAT THEY ARE THINKING and WHO THEY ARE. Paying Attention can Pay Dividends and supports Continual Success.

Inattentiveness can only create Sunk Costs and supports Inconsistent Results."

Thinkable Thoughts and Reflections

Reflecting Upon

PAYING ATTENTION

"The simple act of paying attention can take you a long way."
— **Keanu Reeves**
   A Canadian actor/Born in Beirut and raised in Toronto/ Made his feature film debut in *Youngblood.*

The very first step to *learning* is paying attention. Whether in the classroom, reading a textbook, listening to a podcast, or practicing a skill for work, dedicating complete attention is absolutely critical. What's revealed when you are really paying attention can be the difference between success and failure.

Your Thoughts...

_____

_____

_____

_____

_____

_____

_____

_____

PERFECTIONISTS

"If you are a Perfectionist, get over it. As Human Beings, the reality is, we are all far from perfect. In fact, most experts agree --- *'How the human brain works is flawed and prone to error.'*

Anchoring, Optimism Bias and Herd Mentality are just a few of the most common flaws.

With this in mind, you can aim for perfection in yourself, but do not lament or be constrained by the mediocrity of others."

Thinkable Thoughts and Reflections

Reflecting Upon
PERFECTIONISTS

"People call me a perfectionist, but I'm not. I'm a rightist. I do something until it's right, and then I move on to the next thing."
— James Cameron
  A Canadian filmmaker/Best known for making science fiction and epic films/ First gained recognition for directing *The Terminator*.

Research has demonstrated that perfectionism can lead to significant mental health consequences such as depression, general anxiety, lower life satisfaction, and feelings of low self-worth. Also, unfortunately, perfectionism — takes no prisoners.

Your Thoughts...

_____

_____

_____

_____

_____

_____

_____

_____

_____

GREED AND INSIGHT

"Greed can be a Valuable Human Trait. A Selfish and Excessive Desire for More can be a powerful Motivator and Success Factor.

The key is to consciously balance Selfishness with Courtesy, Civility and Compassionate Restraint. Also, you must view others as worthy competitors and not as adversaries.

Under the right circumstances, self-interest is an inevitable or desirable Human State that can Produce Positive Outcomes."

Thinkable Thoughts and Reflections

Reflecting Upon
GREED AND INSIGHT

"Fear and greed are potent motivators. When both of these forces push in the same direction, virtually no human being can resist."
— Andrew Weil

An American celebrity doctor who advocates for alternative medicine including the 4-7-8 breathing technique.

Fear and greed are the two primal emotions that have propelled human civilization. But, of course, both also have their dark side. Greed is positive and productive when channeled toward personal and professional improvement. However, it turns ugly in pursuit of a single-minded or selfish outcome.

Your Thoughts...

_____

_____

_____

_____

_____

_____

_____

_____

THE SMALL STUFF

"Sweating the Small Stuff can sometimes provide Big Insights. Many have adopted the belief that the time spent worrying about minor things is usually disproportionate to their importance.

Yet, we are also aware of the idiom, *'The Devil is in the details.'*

Minor things can trigger insecurities, issues and wounds that can be blocking opportunities.

Cleverly fretting the Small Stuff can reveal Hidden Obstacles to Vital Victories in life."

Thinkable Thoughts and Reflections

Reflecting Upon
THE SMALL STUFF

"It's the little details that are vital. Little things make big things happen."
— John Wooden

An American basketball coach and player. Nicknamed the "Wizard of Westwood"/Won ten National Collegiate Athletic Association National championships in a 12-year period as head coach for the UCLA Bruins.

The phrase "Don't sweat the small stuff" encourages us to let go of things that aren't important in the grand scheme of our life. However, being aware of the details is important. This learned art sits somewhere between a soft skill and a hard skill, and can be paramount regardless of your position in life.

Your Thoughts...

_____

_____

_____

_____

_____

_____

_____

_____

_____

CRISIS AND CHARACTER

"What should you do when you find yourself in a personal or professional crisis? Of course, you should maintain a level head, be positive and stay calm.

However, your actual response will depend on your Character, which includes your personality, reliability and honesty.

Surfacing unharmed will not only depend upon your level of preparedness, but also your recovery. Remember, the Recovery Process can take time. Be patient."

Thinkable Thoughts and Reflections

Reflecting Upon

CRISIS AND CHARACTER

"Good character is not formed in a week or a month. It is created little by little, day by day. Protracted and patient effort is needed to develop good character."
— Heraclitus

Heraclitus of Ephesus was an ancient Greek, pre-Socratic, Ionian philosopher and a native of the city of Ephesus, of the Persian Empire.

Any sudden and unexpected event leading to major unrest can become a crisis. A crisis affects an individual, group, organization or society on the whole. We cannot be fully prepared for every crisis. However, there are always decisions and actions we can take to minimize the impact.

Your Thoughts...

_____

_____

_____

_____

_____

_____

_____

_____

_____

PUBLIC ERRORS

"You should quickly correct Public Errors that personally or professionally are about you.

Once Errors like these are Widely Broadcasted and not corrected, they become the 'First Impression From Hell' and will always Prevail --- in the minds of some.

Now and then, it will require you to seem out of character.

However, this is a very necessary and proactive part of Telling Your Own Story and self-preservation."

Thinkable Thoughts and Reflections

Reflecting Upon
Public Errors

"He who knows nothing is closer to the truth than he whose mind is filled with falsehoods and errors."
— Thomas Jefferson

An American statesman, diplomat, philosopher, and Founding Father who served as the third president of the United States.

Your reputation is important. Unfortunately, your reputation and public image can be tarnished by the careless or intentionally slanderous words of another. If someone has made a false or harmful statement about you that hurts your reputation address the issue quickly. Unaddressed lies can soon be viewed by others as the truth.

Your Thoughts...

_____

_____

_____

_____

_____

_____

_____

_____

_____

Level of Literacy

"A Socially Conscious Education is more than the acquisition of Knowledge and Intellectual Development. This coveted Level of Literacy can promote Tolerance and Understanding beyond Our Political, Cultural and Religious differences.

A Public-Spirited community, coupled with an honestly Empathetic sense of Humanity can become an Authentic Cure for the lack of Civil Discourse and Destructive Divisiveness."

Reflecting Upon
Level of Literacy

"The key to growth is the introduction of higher dimensions of consciousness into our awareness."
— Lao Tzu
 An Ancient Chinese philosopher and writer.

Social literacy plays a significant role in reducing gender, race, nationality, and religious inequality that favors one group over another in access to education, property, employment, health care, legal, and civic participation. It is a skill that is never too late to acquire or expand.

Your Thoughts...

_____

_____

_____

_____

_____

_____

_____

_____

_____

PUBLIC ARGUMENTS

"Never Argue in Public. There are No Winners. Only Losers. Argumentative, Aggressive and Confrontational behavior can only be Viewed by Strangers as an obvious Lack of Maturity and Emotional Intelligence.

Regardless of who the Other Person is, you will become a Victim of Dual Identity. Why you ask? Because no one will be able to Distinguish a 'Material Difference' between You and the Other Person."

Thinkable Thoughts and Reflections

Reflecting Upon

PUBLIC ARGUMENTS

"You can't win an argument. You can't because if you lose it, you lose it; and if you win it, you lose it."
— Dale Carnegie

An American writer and lecturer, and the developer of courses in self-improvement, salesmanship, corporate training, public speaking, and interpersonal skills.

Unfortunately, most arguments result into heated and angry exchanges of diverging or opposite views void of any listening. Arguing in public shows a lack of self-respect and lack of respect for the other party. It often **leaves both parties feeling lousy and resentful.**

Your Thoughts...

_____

_____

_____

_____

_____

_____

_____

_____

_____

SHOWING UP

"Showing Up is more than half the battle. Truly Showing Up means being <u>present</u> with your <u>presence</u>. It means being in a meeting or in someone's life when you are most needed.

It means being fully equipped with your skills, knowledge, compassion, empathy, spirit, and a willingness to both listen as well as to 'unconditionally' share.

Your presence is more than your existence. It is the Innermost part of who you are, and the pinnacle of your being."

Thinkable Thoughts and Reflections

Reflecting Upon
SHOWING UP

"Eighty percent of success is showing up."
— Woody Allen

   An American film director, writer, actor, and comedian whose career spans more than six decades and multiple Academy Award-winning films.

Showing up means being prepared to put in the work, regardless of outside factors or obstacles, including our own negative self-talk. Showing up with your presence can lead to success by enabling you to reach your fullest potential.

Your Thoughts...

_____

_____

_____

_____

_____

_____

_____

_____

_____

PONDER, BUT VERIFY

"Listen to the Voice in your Head.

But with caution. This Self-Talk is more than just pondering over your own thoughts. It consists of inner speech in your mind. It is completely natural.

But remember that the Mind first chooses Intuition, and not Conscious Reasoning.

Thus, you should always ponder, but verify. Not all your Self-Talk will pass the commonsense test.

At times, Self-Talk can contain errors that may be detrimental and injurious to yourself and others."

Thinkable Thoughts and Reflections

Reflecting Upon
PONDER, BUT VERIFY

"If you do not conquer self, you will be conquered by self."
—Napoleon Hill

An American self-help author. He is best known for his book *Think and Grow Rich.*

The voice in our head or self-talk is the running dialogue we have with ourselves. At times, it can reflect the thinking traps or cognitive distortions that can cause us to miss certain cues or information about a situation. Thinking traps are common, especially in stressful situations. This is why we should take the time to frequently *flush out* thoughts that are not consistent with who we really are.

Your Thoughts...

_____

_____

_____

_____

_____

_____

_____

_____

_____

A Gold Mine

"Let's not confuse Emotions with Emotional Intelligence. One is a natural. The other is a source of wealth and information. Emotions are reactions that we experience in response to situations.

Emotional intelligence is our ability to recognize emotion, reason with emotion, and process emotional information. Emotionally Reacting to life experiences is instigated by Nature.

Strengthening your ability to recognize, reason and positively process your emotions, and the emotions of others, must be instigated by You...and can be a gold mine."

Thinkable Thoughts and Reflections

Reflecting Upon
A GOLD MINE

"Some of the greatest moments in human history were fueled by emotional intelligence."
— **Adam Grant**

An American popular science author, and professor at the Wharton School of the University of Pennsylvania specializing in organizational psychology.

Our brains are physically set up to integrate emotions into how we process information and make decisions. The brain's limbic system is involved in processing, integrating, and regulating emotions. Emotional intelligence includes self-awareness, self-management, and social and relational awareness.

Your Thoughts...

_____

_____

_____

_____

_____

_____

_____

_____

_____

TIME AS YOUR FRIEND

"Making Time your Friend involves Conquering the Three P's --- Procrastination, Prioritization and Planning.

Being consciously Proactive will Phase out Procrastination. Concentrating on the Most Crucial will Promote Prioritization.

Thinking on Paper will put an Edge on your Planning skills.

Just as Friendship is essential to the Soul, Conquering the three P's can be essential to Success in your career and your life."

Thinkable Thoughts and Reflections

Reflecting Upon
TIME AS YOUR FRIEND

"Know the true value of time; snatch, seize, and enjoy every moment of it. No idleness, no laziness, no procrastination: never put off till tomorrow what you can do today."
— Philip Stanhope, 4th Earl of Chesterfield
   A British statesman, diplomat, and man of letters, and an acclaimed wit of his time.

There are ways you can make time your friend, rather than your archenemy. If you work according to your natural pace, be content with what you manage to accomplish and establish a work/life balance that will establish a foundation for effectively managing your time.

Your Thoughts...

_____

_____

_____

_____

_____

_____

_____

_____

Worst Lies

"The Worst Lies are the Lies you Tell Yourself. Lying has Consequences. When Others find out you have Lied, it affects how they Deal with you Forever.

When you Realize that a Lie has come out of your Mouth, premeditatively or mistakenly, you Must Deal with the Lie and Yourself.

And it gets even worst.

The Second Lie You Tell Yourself to be Convinced the First lie was OK, can start a chain of Destructive Deception."

Reflecting Upon
Worst Lies

"The most common lie is that which one lies to himself; lying to others is relatively an exception."
— Friedrich Nietzsche

A German philosopher, cultural critic and philologist whose work has exerted a profound influence on modern intellectual history.

There are many types of lies we may tell others. Some are innocent and may be small and insignificant. Some may be damaging. But the worst lies are the ones we tell ourselves. Because we easily start living in the illusion of being someone we are not, doing things we don't really like, fearing things that can never actually happen, and much more.

Your Thoughts...

_____

_____

_____

_____

_____

_____

_____

_____

_____

Ignorance

"As you might know, there is a significant difference in Being Stupid and Being Ignorant. Being Stupid infers a Lack of intelligence, while Being Ignorant implies a Lack of Knowledge.

In today's information rich society, most instances of personal or professional Ignorance – is a Choice.

It is a Choice which is instinctively obvious to others and deprives you from being the Best You and making the Best Decisions.

Just as Honesty, Confidence, Creativity and a Positive Attitude are considered your "Friends", when it comes to Good Decision-Making, ignorance becomes your Worst Enemy."

Thinkable Thoughts and Reflections

Reflecting Upon

Ignorance

"Real knowledge is to know the extent of one's ignorance."
— **Confucius**
   A Chinese philosopher and politician of the Spring and Autumn period.

There are two types of ignorance. The first category of ignorance is when we do not know we are ignorant. This is primary ignorance. The second category of ignorance is when we recognize our ignorance and choose to not become more knowledgeable regarding the topic or issue. This can be called "veiled ignorance" when other motives or desires are at hand.

Your Thoughts...

_____

_____

_____

_____

_____

_____

_____

_____

_____

Resilience

"Whether from misfortune, bad luck, hardship or other difficulties, Adversity can either Sharpen or Obscure the normal senses that the brain uses to help us understand and accurately perceive situations and more positive outcomes.

Possessing a healthy dose of Resilience – through Mental, Emotional and Behavioral Flexibility – can be a formidable Weapon in fighting Obscurity.

This process will allow you to make the required adjustments, give you the edge needed to choose from available paths, and help you realize a Positive Recovery more quickly."

Thinkable Thoughts and Reflections

Reflecting Upon
Resilience

"Resilience isn't a single skill. It's a variety of skills and coping mechanisms. To bounce back from bumps in the road as well as failures, you should focus on emphasizing the positive."
— Jean Chatzky

   An American journalist, a personal finance columnist, financial editor of NBC's TODAY show, and the founder and CEO of the multimedia company *Her Money*.

When we have resilience, we harness the inner strength that helps us rebound from a setback or challenge. It will not make our problems go away. However, resilience can strengthen our ability to put problems in perspective and achieve better outcomes.

Your Thoughts...

_____

_____

_____

_____

_____

_____

_____

_____

Funny and Frightful

"Fear is Funny and Frightful. It is Funny because the very instinct designed to Protect Us also Holds Us Back. It is Frightful because it is the only human emotion that consistently causes unpleasant, serious, or even shocking life episodes.

However, because Fear is a natural, powerful, and primitive emotion, which alerts us to the presence of danger or the threat of harm, it is a survival mechanism that we should learn how to systematically control, conquer and take advantage of."

Thinkable Thoughts and Reflections

Reflecting Upon
Funny and Frightful

"The oldest and strongest emotion of mankind is fear, and the oldest and strongest kind of fear is fear of the unknown."
— H. P. Lovecraft
　An American writer of weird, science, fantasy, and horror fiction.

Fear is a primitive emotion that we have as humans. Fear is used to tell us about the danger that might be around us. There are two different types of reactions to fear — *biochemical* and *emotional* reactions. Increased heart rate, sweating, and higher adrenaline levels are biochemical responses. Emotional responses may be felt as a positive or negative experience or encounter.

Your Thoughts...

_____

_____

_____

_____

_____

_____

_____

_____

_____

Caution and Doubt

"As you know, Caution helps to avoid danger and mistakes while Doubt seeks honest conviction. But did you know that Caution and Doubt work together to enable Deep Thought and Introspection.

Both of which are the two main ingredients in the recipe for gaining Understanding Beyond Measure."

Thinkable Thoughts and Reflections

Reflecting Upon
Caution and Doubt

"The truth. It is a beautiful and terrible thing, and must therefore be treated with great caution."
— J. K. Rowling

   Joanne Rowling is a British author and philanthropist/She wrote *Harry Potter*, a seven-volume children's fantasy series.

Caution and doubt can work together. However, there is a distinct difference between them. *Caution* might require taking safety precautions before embarking on a task, while *doubt* literally says "no." However, it is possible for doubt to be transformed into caution with more introspection and understanding.

Your Thoughts...

_____

_____

_____

_____

_____

_____

_____

_____

_____

SIGNIFICANCE OF THE VEIL

"Many of us Misunderstand the Significance of the 'Veil' during crucial conversations with others. The idea of Veiling or Concealing Portions of your Thoughts and Opinions until the Opportune moment is not Disingenuous.

It is actually Ingenuous.

The sheer Simplicity of this crafty Communications Skill allows you to do two things. The First is to gain Valuable Insights on the topic from their perspective, and Secondly, it prevents you from becoming too entrenched in your Initial Thoughts prior to gaining a Broader Perspective."

Thinkable Thoughts and Reflections

Reflecting Upon

SIGNIFICANCE OF THE VEIL

"There was a door to which I found no key: There was the veil through which I might not see."
— Omar Khayyam

A polymath, known for his contributions to mathematics, astronomy, philosophy, and Persian poetry.

An Interesting Note: Social Theories draw energy not just from the concepts that the "veil" articulates but also from the images it invokes. Unlike the mask, which suggests a binary account of human conduct (what is covered can be uncovered), the veil summons a wide range of human experiences. From the veil's association with religion to its symbolism of material culture.

Your Thoughts...

_____

_____

_____

_____

_____

_____

_____

_____

_____

RETIREMENT

"When you Retire and Exit the work you once loved So Dear, don't be disappointed when the Voices and Faces of former co-workers also Disappear.

Just recall that while enjoying your work, you were also eagerly engaged in the two activities required to ensure career success. Looking for New Opportunities that would support promotions and more respect, while spending your Free Time looking to see who Had or who Wanted your back.

Hence, hearing from or seeing former co-workers less and less...just means that they are busy...ensuring Their Success."

Thinkable Thoughts and Reflections

Reflecting Upon

RETIREMENT

"Preparation for old age should begin no later than one's teens. A life which is empty of purpose until 65 will not suddenly become filled on retirement."
— Dwight L. Moody
   An American evangelist and publisher, who founded the Moody Church.

Retirement is a major life event. As we age, we gain valuable experiences and insights – worthy of being shared. But every day, millions of older adults struggle with challenges such as declining health, the loss of loved ones, and feelings of isolation. Developing meaningful connections during retirement can improve health and well-being.

Your Thoughts...

_____

_____

_____

_____

_____

_____

_____

_____

_____

JOY AND HAPPINESS

"Choosing Joy over Happiness is a Tough Call. As we all know, Happiness is an emotion that allows us to experience meaningful bursts of Satisfaction and Pleasure. While Joy is a Stronger, less common feeling, that provides the much sought-after inward peace and contentment.

Why is it such a Tough Call?

Because when you think of Happiness as a tall Building with each floor representing increasing levels of 'Being Happy', you must also think of Joy as being the Elevator that makes it convenient to get to the higher levels. Therefore, Happiness wrapped in Joy should be the Ultimate Goal."

Thinkable Thoughts and Reflections

Reflecting Upon

JOY AND HAPPINESS

"Happiness is there for the taking — and making."
— **Oprah Winfrey**

An American talk show host, television producer, actress, author, and philanthropist.

Many of us spend our days seeking happiness. However, joy is a much more enduring feeling that persists regardless of the situation. Happiness can broaden our thinking in ways that make us more flexible and more creative. Joy boosts our immune systems, fights stress and pain, and improves our chance of living a longer life. Together they give us fleeting episodes of pleasure along with a deep and lifelong feeling of contentment.

Your Thoughts...

_____

_____

_____

_____

_____

_____

_____

_____

_____

About The Authors

Charlotte D. Grant-Cobb, PhD

Charlotte is a gifted author, change management coach, professional mentor and author. She is an International Coaching Federation (ICF) Certified Coach.

Charlotte's extensive resume includes over 30 years of professional accomplishment. She has held senior leadership positions within Fortune 100 corporations, small business enterprises as well as in Federal and State government.

She earned her Bachelor of Science degree in Management and a Master of Business Administration degree from *Arizona State University*. She also earned a professional Doctor of Philosophy in Nutrition Counseling degree from *LaSalle University*.

Charlotte uses her gifts to help her clients gain new awareness, create new habits, forge new pathways and embrace new experiences.

About The Authors

Ervin (Earl) Cobb

Earl is an accomplished corporate executive, leadership development coach, lecturer, and author. He is currently the CEO & Managing Partner of Richer Life, LLC.

Earl has held senior technical and leadership positions within Fortune 100, Mid-market and Venture companies including *Honeywell, Inc., Motorola, Inc., The Reynolds and Reynolds Company* and *Wells Fargo Bank.* He is the former President, COO and CEO of the high-tech start-up, *MedContrax, Inc.*

He earned a Bachelor of Science degree in Electrical Engineering, with honors, from *Tennessee State University.* He graduated from *Arizona State University* with a Master of Science degree in Engineering.

Earl is a former Adjunct Professor of Management at the Keller Graduate School of Management of *DeVry University.* He has completed graduate studies at *Stanford University's Graduate School of Business, the Sloan School of Management at MIT* and the *Center for Creative Leadership.*

www.ingramcontent.com/pod-product-compliance
Lightning Source LLC
Chambersburg PA
CBHW050821090426
42737CB00022B/3462